CONTENTS

Words in **bold** are in the glossary.

WHAT IS GYMNASTICS?

Do you like to flip? Do you like to test your **balance**? Gymnastics may be the sport for you! Gymnasts spin and twist. They balance and swing. They move their bodies in amazing ways. You can be a gymnast too!

Please return or renew this item by the last date shown.

Libraries Line and Renewals: **020 7361 3010**

Web Renewals: www.rbkc.gov.uk/renewyourbooks

KENSINGTON AND CHELSEA LIBRARY SERVICE

Raintree is an imprint of Capstone Global Library Limited, a company incorporated in England and Wales having its registered office at 264 Banbury Road, Oxford, OX2 7DY – Registered company number: 6695582

www.raintree.co.uk
myorders@raintree.co.uk

Edited by Shelly Lyons
Designed by Tracy McCabe
Original illustrations © Capstone Global Library Limited 2021
Picture research by Svetlana Zhurkin
Production by Laura Manthe
Originated by Capstone Global Library Ltd
Printed and bound in India

978 1 3982 0338 9 (hardback)
978 1 3982 0337 2 (paperback)

British Library Cataloguing in Publication Data
A full catalogue record for this book is available from the British Library.

Acknowledgements
We would like to thank the following for permission to reproduce photographs: Dreamstime: Igokapil, 11; Getty Images: Corbis/Tim Clayton, 6, 7, 8, 16; iStockphoto: vgajic, 13; Shutterstock: advent, back cover, 1, ArtMari, cover (balance beam), Erickson Stock, 19, Jiang Dao Hua, cover (girl), Leonard Zhukovsky, 5, Master1305, 15, 17, Michael C. Gray, 14, 21, Patty Chan (background), cover, back cover, and throughout, sportpoint, 9

Every effort has been made to contact copyright holders of material reproduced in this book. Any omissions will be rectified in subsequent printings if notice is given to the publisher.

All the internet addresses (URLs) given in this book were valid at the time of going to press. However, due to the dynamic nature of the internet, some addresses may have changed, or sites may have changed or ceased to exist since publication. While the author and publisher regret any inconvenience this may cause readers, no responsibility for any such changes can be accepted by either the author or the publisher.

Gymnasts perform **routines** at **events**. Each routine is worth a number of points. Difficult skills are worth more points. Mistakes mean points are taken away.

Teams compete at a **meet**. Judges watch routines. Then they give scores. Each person's score is added to the team's total. The team with the most points wins.

WHAT DO I NEED?

Gymnasts do routines on vault and floor. Girls also have balance beam and uneven bars. Boys have parallel bars, pommel horse, still rings and high bar too.

leotard

grips

Boys and girls wear uniforms for meets. Girls wear **leotards**. Boys wear leotards with shorts or stirrup trousers. Grips and chalk are needed for hands.

WHERE DO I GO?

Practices and meets take place in gyms. Gyms are found at clubs or schools. Club gyms have gymnastics equipment. They have classes and teams you can join. Some schools also have teams. Most school teams have a short season.

HOW DO I LEARN?

Coaches help you to learn gymnastics. They **spot** you to keep you safe while learning new skills. Never try skills that are too hard for you. Always make sure someone is there to spot you when learning new skills. Soon you will master the skill.

13

Before doing skills, you warm up and stretch. You do exercises to get strong. You work on getting **flexible**. This will help you to do skills safely.

Some skills are easier than others. You learn the easy skills first. To learn a skill, you must do it many times. Many skills put together make up a routine.

Each event needs different skills. You can compete at one or all events. Floor exercise has flips and dance moves. Bars have swinging skills. Rings have strength skills. Beam has balance skills. For vault, you need speed and power.

HOW CAN I BE A GOOD SPORT?

It can take a long time to learn gymnastics skills. Everyone learns at a different speed. Keep trying. Help others to try hard too.

Be a good sport in the gym. Listen to your coach. Take turns. Cheer for your teammates. Tell other team members they are doing well too. Smile and have fun!

SKILL BUILDER: DOING A HANDSTAND

A handstand is a basic gymnastics skill. To master it, you need strength, balance and good form. Practise a handstand with an adult who can spot you. Follow these simple steps.

1. Start in a lunge position with your arms up. Put your stronger leg in front. Your knee should not be over your ankle. To help with balance, keep your eyes on something in front of you.

2. Kick up to a handstand. Keep your legs together. To keep your body as straight as possible, make sure you squeeze your bottom. Don't forget to point your toes!

3. If you lose your balance and start to fall backwards, just tuck your head and do a roll.

4. To return to a standing position, bring one leg down at a time.

GLOSSARY

balance ability to keep steady and not fall over

event part of a meet where gymnasts perform on a specific piece of equipment

flexible able to bend or move easily

leotard snug, one-piece clothing item worn by female gymnasts

meet contest between teams

routine set of skills that a gymnast performs for an event

spot assist and keep close watch on someone performing a skill

FIND OUT MORE

BOOKS

Floor Exercise: Tips, Rules and Legendary Stars, Heather E. Schwartz (Raintree, 2017)

Gymnastics (First Sport), James Nixon (Franklin Watts, 2016)

Gymnastics (Usborne Spectator Guides), Sam Lake and Emily Bone (Usborne, 2016)

WEBSITES

www.bbc.com/bitesize/articles/z36j7ty

www.british-gymnastics.org

www.dkfindout.com/uk/sports/gymnastics

INDEX